THE STONES OF VENICE

THE STONES OF
VENICE

JULIE LAWSON

SCOTTISH NATIONAL PORTRAIT GALLERY
1992

Published by the Trustees
of the National Galleries of Scotland
for the exhibition at the Scottish National Portrait Gallery
26 November 1992 to 14 March 1993
ISBN 0 903598 30 2

—

Plates 6, 8 & 14 are photographs from a private collection.
All other plates are photographs from the Riddell Collection in the
Scottish National Portrait Gallery.
The figure illustrations are reproduced by permission of the
National Library of Scotland.

—

Printed by Balding & Mansell, Wisbech
Designed & typeset by Dalrymple in Monotype Centaur
based on the fifteenth-century Venetian types of Nicolas Jenson
and the chancery italics of Lodovico degli Arrighi
The device on the title page is a
Venetian arabesque of
1552

John Ruskin regarded Venice as a city in some ways bereft of its history, yet of such loveliness that every stone served as a record of the spirit of the countless artists and craftsmen who had made it. He looked at this city with eyes unequalled in their ability to register both its detail and its accumulated substance. In his heroic attempt to attain to the essence of the place, he recorded Venice in a prose of singular particularity and in drawings of great beauty. What he was able to express of his vision would have a profound effect on all those subsequent travellers to the city who made the attempt to unravel something of the meaning of its unique magic.

In his quest for the stages of growth of this water-encompassed city, Ruskin made careful use of the relatively new art of photography, an art which would rapidly lead to countless images for an ever-growing market of tourists. Among those photographers working in Venice at the same time as Ruskin and who saw, in their own way, something of the same city that he saw, were Carlo Naya and Carlo Ponti. Their photographs illustrate this publication which aims to bring both Ruskin and the Venice he knew into a focus that will illuminate one of the, we hope, eternal wonders of Europe.

The publication also serves as a companion to an exhibition of Naya's and Ponti's photographs of Venice held at the Scottish National Portrait Gallery in December 1992 to celebrate the Edinburgh meeting, under Britain's presidency, of the heads of government of the European Community.

Timothy Clifford
Director · National Galleries of Scotland

Duncan Thomson
Keeper · Scottish National Portrait Gallery

I N 'THE STONES OF VENICE', WHICH WAS PUBLISHED IN THREE VOLUMES BETWEEN 1851 AND 1853, JOHN RUSKIN PROPOSED TO RECONCILE WHAT HE LATER CAME TO SEE AS INCOMPATIBLE CONCERNS: aesthetics and political philosophy. Its basic premise was that Venetian art and architecture could be seen as an embodiment and expression of the political and religious history of the city, and the moral character of its inhabitants. Ruskin believed that there is a sense in which the stones of the buildings of Venice could, like any other document, be 'read' for their revelations about the people who built them: their values, beliefs, and aspirations.

The story they would tell was a tragic one. Venice was, for Ruskin, a dead place. The book is both a valediction and a memorial — a record of the city which would eventually be drowned beneath the very sea she once dominated. It was also quite explicitly intended as an admonition and a warning to that other Empire whose proud boast was that she 'ruled the waves'.

Ruskin lays both his thesis and his purpose before the reader in the first passage of the book: '*Since first the dominion of men was asserted over the ocean, three thrones, of mark beyond all others, have been set upon its sands: the thrones of Tyre, Venice and England. Of the First of these great powers only the memory remains; of the Second, the ruin; the Third, which inherits their greatness, if it forget their example, may be led through prouder eminence to less pitied destruction ...*' Venice '*is still left for our beholding in the final period of her decline: a ghost upon the sands of the sea, so weak — so quiet — so bereft of all but her loveliness, that we might well doubt, as we watched her faint reflection in the mirage of the lagoon, which was the City, and which the Shadow. I would endeavour to trace the lines of this image before it be forever lost, and to record, as far as I may, the warning which seems to me to be uttered by every one of the fast-gaining waves, that beat like passing bells, against the Stones of Venice.*'

The development — and in Ruskin's terms decline — of the architectural styles which are represented in the buildings of Venice, both parallels and illustrates the greatness, decline and fall of the nation state. Whereas Gibbon had accounted for another Decline and Fall in the lofty terms of constitutional enfeeblement and forces of unreason within and without, Ruskin found his cause in terms, finally, of the alienation of the human heart from the hand and from the head. In contemporary political terms the message of *The Stones of Venice* was clear to see. Ruskin stated that his purpose in choosing to write what might aptly be seen as an extended 'sermon in stones', was to point the moral lesson before it was too late. He was, before long, to give up writing about art in order to concentrate upon social and economic matters, believing that he could not in conscience concern himself with art, when the evidence of 'evil' in the form of poverty and despair were all around him. Venice was chosen as the object of his study, because it was, like Britain, a great maritime and mercantile power. It had fallen from greatness, he argued, through a fatal combination of materialism, godlessness, and the misuse of power by a corrupt and incompetent oligarchy.

Ruskin's is a kind of inverted Vasarian view of the history of art. He replaces the model of birth, growth, maturity and fruition, with that of youth, innocence and purity of spirit, followed by inevitable corruption, decadence and decay. Vasari found perfection in the apogee of the Renaissance, the art of Michelangelo. This Renaissance concept of perfectibility is what Ruskin found so antipathetic. It typified, for him, the pride and arrogance of the Renaissance – a repetition of the sin of Adam which led to another lost Eden. Where there is perfectibility, can authority and orthodoxy be far behind? Ruskin's preference was always for nascent styles, both in architecture and painting. He preferred the painting of Giovani Bellini, for the purity of its religious sentiment, to the painting of Titian – unsurpassed as far as 'mere art' was concerned but, for Ruskin, tainted with the materialism which he regarded as a symptom of the corrupting influence of the Renaissance.

Ruskin preferred early Gothic architecture to the 'straight-jacket' of English perpendicular and what he scathingly called 'Confectioner's Gothic', exemplified by King's College Chapel in Cambridge – a regulated, and therefore self-contradictory, form of Gothic architecture. The painting that exemplified his love of early Italian Renaissance art was Carpaccio's *Dream of St Ursula* in the Accademia in Venice. Its subject matter – the piety of a virgin saint – was perfectly married with the style, whose clarity, simplicity, economy of means, and lack of ostentation were, Ruskin felt, beyond praise. Painting had not yet become a vehicle for that other Promethean folly of the Renaissance, 'genius'. In Ruskin's scheme of things, 'after the Byzantine Spring and Gothic summer, Autumn came – the leaves were shed – and the eye was directed to the extremities of the delicate branches. The Renaissance frosts came, and all perished!'

Ruskin's basic thesis is the superiority, in both aesthetic and moral terms, of Gothic over Classical architecture. He argues this in various ways, and the styles are characterised and discussed in great depth. A definition of the Gothic style was complex, since 'every building of the Gothic period differs in some important respect from every other'. The lack of uniformity was one of its essential characteristics. So it was 'Gothicness' that was to be sought in buildings. Ruskin discoverd it not only in the Ducal Palace, the 'central building of the world', but in obscure and isolated details. 'One of the richest fragments in the city' was to be found, for example, in the windows of 'a small palace, modernized in all its other parts' in the Campo Sta. Maria Mater Domini *(below)*.

In *The Stones of Venice*, Ruskin condemns Classical architecture as 'haughty' and arrogant in its austerity and clarity. It pretends, he argues, to offer perfection to the beholder, with the reduction of its elements to basic geometrical forms – 'a few clear and forceful lines'. In contrast, it is the Christian virtue of 'Humility' that is 'the very life of the Gothic school'. Paradoxically, it is this very imperfection or 'rude-ness', finding its best expression in the 'accumulation of ornament', that is praiseworthy. Ornament is, for Ruskin, that aspect of architecture that makes it art; it is the non-essential, non-functional, 're-dundant' part of a building. In the work of the medieval masons he sees 'a magnificent enthusiasm, which feels as if it never could do enough to reach the fullness of its ideal'. The attitude of 'unselfishness of sacrifice' results in 'fruitless labour' (invis-

Arabian Windows in Campo Santa Mater Domini
Lithograph by Thomas Lumpton after a drawing by John Ruskin

ible, for the most part, to any observer not perched on top of a very tall ladder), and this profligacy of effort is also, for Ruskin, of inestimable value.

Ruskin spent much of his time in Venice up one ladder or another. By this means he was able, quite literally, to see more than any previous commentator on the monuments of the city. In the church of SS Giovanni e Paolo, for example, he was able to announce triumphantly that his low opinion of the sculptor of the Renaissance tomb of Doge Andrea Vendramin was confirmed, because the far side of the prostrate figure – seen normally from below and one side – had not been carved at all. Worse still, he discovered that the figure only had one hand. (Ruskin felt further vindicated when he read in the Venetian archives that the sculptor who had perpetrated this act of gross deception had been banished from Venice for forgery in 1487. He is subsequently referred to by Ruskin as the 'convict, Tullio Lombardo'.) Ruskin's writing on art was imbued with the Protestant work ethic – instilled in him by his Scottish parents – and elaborated by him into an aesthetic theory.

Ruskin argued for the superiority of Gothic over Classical architecture in straight-forward religious as well as moral terms. The greatest virtue of Gothic ornamentation was that it gave evidence of a 'profound sympathy with the fullness and wealth of the material universe' – a love of Nature. This was not crude materialism, but a recognition that Nature, in its plenitude and variety, was God's self-expression in temporal and material terms. To delight in and imitate Nature was, then, a spiritual exercise – an act of worship.

The 'vine angle' of the Ducal Palace, Ruskin wrote *'is a remarkable instance of the Gothic Naturalism; and, indeed, it is almost impossible for the copying of nature to be carried further than in the fibres of the marble branches, and the careful finishing of the tendrils: note especially the peculiar expression of the knotty joints of the vine in the light branch which rises highest. Yet only half the finish of the work can be seen in the Plate [below]: for, in several cases, the sculptor has shown the under sides of the leaves turned boldly to the light, and has literally carved every rib and vein upon them in relief; not merely the main ribs which sustain the lobes of the leaf, and actually project in nature, but the irregular and sinuous veins which chequer the membranous tissues between them, and which the sculptor has represented conventionally as relieved like the others, in order to give the vine-leaf its peculiar tessellated effect upon the eye.'*

Truth to nature was perhaps Ruskin's most abiding concern. It recurs like a *leitmotif* throughout his writings on art. The precept is expressed in *Modern Painters* in his famous exhortation to painters to abandon their sterile academicism and see afresh through their own eyes instead of those of Raphael and his imitators, dulled with time and tired with use. In *The Stones of Venice* Ruskin wrote: *'The sculptor who sought for his models among the forest leaves, could not but quickly and deeply feel that complexity need not involve the loss of grace, nor richness that of repose; ... and where he saw throughout the universe a faultless beauty lavished on measureless spaces of broidered field and blooming mountain, [he could not] grudge his poor and imperfect labour to the few stones that he had raised one upon another, for habitation or memorial ... and the cathedral front was at last lost in the tapestry of its traceries, like a rock among the thickets and herbage of spring.'*

Leafage of the Vine Angle e*ngraved by J. C. Armytage after a drawing by John Ruskin, illustration to* The Stones of Venice

The crux of his argument is that the condition necessary for the making of Classical architecture is that of slavery. Classical buildings require slaves – literally, as in ancient Greece – or metaphorically and virtually, when craftsmen are set to slavish copying and repetitive tasks. It is a building style in which the stone mason is not permitted to use his imagination or powers of invention, and so his work is not a creative exercise. Where heart and head are not equally engaged, argues Ruskin, the resulting condition is one of alienation: the craftsman is reduced to the condition of labourer – a mere functionary. Where there is no freedom, there is a condition of enslavement. The opposite, he proceeds to demonstrate, is true of Gothic architecture.

In his chapter on 'The Nature of Gothic', which is at the heart of the work, Ruskin wrote an impassioned condemnation of the mode of production in which the worker was reduced to the condition of a mere cog in a machine. In a powerful invective against the combination and division of labour he denounces a system of wealth creation that demands that people be 'sent like fuel to feed the factory smoke, and the strength of them is given daily to be wasted into the fineness of a web, or racked into the exactness of a line.'

The following was a direct criticism of Adam Smith's hypothetical pin factory in his *Inquiry into the Nature and Causes of the Wealth of Nations*, the model for the factory system: '*We have much studied and much perfected, of late, the great civilized invention of the division of labour; only we give it a false name. It is not, truly speaking, the labour that is divided; but the men: – Divided into mere segments of men – broken into small fragments and crumbs of life; so that all the little piece of intelligence that is left in a man is not enough to make up a pin, or a nail, but exhausts itself in making the point of a pin or the head of a nail ... And the great cry that rises from all our manufacturing cities, louder than their furnace blast is ... that we manufacture everything there except men.*'

Ruskin instructs his reader to '*go forth again to gaze upon the old cathedral front, where you have smiled so often at the fantastic ignorance of the old sculptors: examine once more those ugly goblins, and formless monsters, and stern statues, anatomiless and rigid; but do not mock at them, for they are signs of the life and liberty of every workman who struck the stone; a freedom of thought, and rank in scale of being, such as no laws, no charters, no charities can secure; but which it must be the first aim of all Europe at this day to regain for her children.*'

The Stones of Venice is unequalled as a study of the city and its architecture. Ruskin's work on St Mark's in particular is exemplary, as an examination of the building and its ornamentation. His method was to examine minutely and look intensely, then to deduce from the visual information what may subsequently be confirmed by

Carlo Ponti *Doorway of a house at the Ponte del Forner with carved tympanum (albumen print).*

Examples of a carved tympanum
From a drawing by John Ruskin, illustration from The Stones of Venice

documentary evidence. The result is an archaeological, aesthetic, iconographical and, ultimately, moral analysis of the architecture.

Ruskin then extrapolates from his findings to the whole of the city and its history. This was only possible because of his belief that architectural styles are both an expression and a reflection of the society in which they came into existence. In this, Ruskin in turn could be said to typify his age; it is difficult to imagine a twentieth century writer being able to preach to his audience in the same terms. Ruskin was heir to the Romantics (though he tried assiduously to rid himself of their influence in some important respects); his love of emergent artistic styles, for example, is symptomatic of this influence on his intellectual and emotional make-up. His views on Gothic architecture and his advocacy of its use in both religious and secular buildings come very close to those of Pugin, though they were arrived at independently. *(see left)*

While, inevitably, a product of his own age and culture, Ruskin anticipates in several respects modern Marxist art historians, not only in the basic philosophical questioning of the forces of capitalism, but in his belief that the study of art and political discourse go hand in hand. Their thinking about the alienation of labour is not dissimilar. *The Stones of Venice* is a polemical work and it contains Ruskin's famous diatribe against the immorality of the capitalist means of production: the essay entitled 'The Nature of Gothic', which William Morris considered one of the 'few necessary and inevitable utterances of the century'.

Ruskin dated 'the commencement of the decline of the Venetian power' very precisely to 1423, and the death of the Doge Tomaso Mocenigo. *The Stones of Venice* ends with an apocalyptic vision of the city in its demise: *'Venice had in her childhood sown, in tears, the harvest she was to reap in rejoicing. She now sowed in laughter the seeds of death ... By the inner burning of her own passions, as fatal as the fiery rain of Gomorrah, she was consumed from her place among the nations; and her ashes are choking the channels of the dead, salt sea'.*

RUSKIN AND PHOTOGRAPHY

Ruskin welcomed the camera as a means of recording both comprehensively and accurately. He used it with enthusiasm in his study of Venetian architecture, virtually as an extension of the art of drawing. He did not regard his own drawings as 'art' — he made no such claims for them. They were, in their making, aids to looking and were, subsequently, aids for memory.

The illustrations to *The Stones of Venice* were all lithographs and mezzotints from Ruskin's own drawings and watercolours. Their chief virtue, he claimed in the prospectus for the book, 'will be their almost servile veracity — a merit which will be appreciated when the buildings themselves are no more; and they perish daily.' He wrote 'I never draw architecture in outline, not unless I can make perfect notes of the forms of its shadows, and foci of its lights.' He described his method of depiction as 'bold Rembrandtism — that is to say [by] the sacrifice of details in the shadowed parts, in order that greater depth of tone might be afforded on the lights'. *(see illustration overleaf)* The tenebrist result so closely resembled a photographic image, that Ruskin felt obliged to add: 'Studies made on such a system if successful, resemble daguerreotypes'; and his illustrations 'have been mistaken by several persons for copies of them'. This, he said, was not the case, 'but I have used the help of the daguerreotype without scruple in completing many of the mezzotint subjects for the present series *[Examples of the Architecture of Venice]* and I much regret that artists in general do not think it worth their while to perpetuate some of the beautiful effects which the daguerreotype alone can seize'.

The question of the authorship of the daguerreotypes taken in Venice is in a sense an irrelevant one. It seems more than likely that Ruskin's servant, John Hobbs, was responsible for the practical aspects, but it is inconceivable that Ruskin would not have directed the photography and have carefully selected the viewpoints. There is even documentary evidence to this effect in the form of a passage in one of Effie Ruskin's letters of 1850, in which she wrote: *'John excites the liveliest astonishment to all and sundry in Venice and I do not think they have made up their minds yet whether he is very mad or very wise. Nothing interrupts him and whether the Square [St Mark's] is crowded or empty he is either seen with a black cloth over his head taking Daguerrotypes [sic] or climbing about the capitals covered with dust.'*

The truthfulness of the daguerreotype is what Ruskin valued most – its ability to render completely and with complete impartiality. In fact, Ruskin found it more

Saint Mark's Southern Portico *Lithograph by T. S. Boys after a drawing by John Ruskin, from* Examples of the Architecture of Venice *1851*

reliable and comprehensive than even his own eagle-eyed scrutiny: he admitted that he discovered things in the daguerreotypes of St Mark's 'that I had never noticed in the place itself'.

The truthfulness of the camera's impartial vision made it superior in some respects to the work of certain artists who met with Ruskin's disapproval because of their perceived inaccuracies. Canaletto, for example, is criticised for his 'miserable, virtueless, heartless mechanism' which Ruskin saw as 'among the most striking signs of the lost sensation and deadened intellect of a nation at that time'. Mechanism – a virtue of the machine – was, for Ruskin, a sin in a man. Canaletto was accused, perhaps unfairly by Ruskin, of distortion of forms and proportions (Canaletto was using optical measuring devices so these should not be inaccurate) suppression of detail and inexactitude of colour. The daguerreotypes on the other hand 'taken by the vivid sunlight are glorious things. It is very nearly the same thing as carrying off the palace itself – every chip and stone and stain is there – and of course there is no mistake about proportions'.

In his autobiographical work, *Praeterita*, Ruskin recalled finding, in Venice, 'a French artist producing exquisitely bright small plates, (about four inches square) which contained, under a lens, the Grand Canal or St Mark's Place as if a magician had reduced the reality to be carried away into an enchanted land. The little gems of pictures cost a napoleon each; but with two hundred francs I bought the Grand Canal from the Salute to the Rialto; and packed it away in thoughtless triumph'. It is tempting to conjecture that Ruskin, himself a former student at Christ Church, Oxford, and friend of Dean Liddell – and subsequently Slade Lecturer at the University – had discussed photography with the mathematics don and amateur photographer, the Rev C. L. Dodgson (Lewis Carroll).

Ruskin's interest in the camera was essentially a utilitarian one. But then, if its role was a humble one, it was that much more to be cherished. Ruskin's system of aesthetic value was, as it were, a rehearsal of the Sermon on the Mount. The painstaking sculptor and the scrupulous observer could have a moral kinship. The Gothic sculptor contributes his labour in such lavish abundance that the human eye cannot grasp the detail. It is the moral sense that grasps the significance of the profligacy of his invention. But the camera – the scrupulous observer – can be thought of as recombining these forms of perception. Being able to see, literally by means of the camera, such endless toil and fantasy, is to be assured of the artist's integrity and joy.

POSTSCRIPT

In this book Ruskin's commentaries are used in conjunction with photographs taken in the 1850s and '60s by Carlo Naya and Carlo Ponti. These photographs should properly be considered as works of great pictorial value in their own right, and the intention is not merely to use them as visual illustrations to Ruskin's texts. On the contrary: just as Ruskin's literary skills and intellectual energies were employed, not for their own sake, but in the service of the place he called 'the paradise of cities', so the beautiful images of Venice made by these photographers are complemented by his observations about their shared subject matter. JL

CARLO NAYA
The west front of St Mark's

'... there rises a vision out of the earth, and all the great square seems to have opened from it in a kind of awe, that we may see it far away — a multitude of pillars and white domes, clustered into a long low pyramid of coloured light; a treasure-heap, it seems, partly of gold, and partly of opal and mother-of-pearl, hollowed beneath into five great vaulted porches, ceiled with fair mosaic, and beset with sculpture of alabaster, clear as amber and delicate as ivory.'

CARLO PONTI

The fourth and fifth porticos of west front of St Mark's

*'St Mark's porches are full of doves, that nestle among the marble foliage, and mingle the soft iri-
descence of their living plumes, changing at every motion, with the tints, hardly less lovely, that have
stood unchanged for seven hundred years.'*

ATTRIBUTED TO CARLO PONTI
Fondaco De'Turchi
Byzantine palace built on the Grand Canal c.1250

'Not only is every one of these capitals differently fancied, but there are many which have no two sides alike ... But this is not all the differences in the ornamentation between them and the Greek capitals: all show a greater love of nature, the leaves are, every one of them, more founded on realities, sketched, however rudely, more directly from the truth, and are continually treated in a manner which shows the mind of the workman to have been among the living herbage, not among the Greek precedents.'

ATTRIBUTED TO CARLO PONTI

Palazzo Cicogna

CARLO PONTI

Evangelist windows of a house at the Ponte del Forner, San Cassano

'When the Gothic feeling began more decidedly to establish itself, it evidently became a question with the Venetian builders how the intervals between the arches, now left blank by the abandonment of the Byzantine sculptures, should be enriched in accordance with the principles of the new school. Two most important examples are left of the experiments made at this period: one of the Ponte del Forner at San Cassano, a noble house in which the spandrils of the windows are filled by the emblems of the four Evangelists, sculptures in deep relief, and touching the edges of the arches with their expanded wings; the other now known as the Palazzo Cicogna, near the Church of S. Sebastiano, in the quarter called "of the Archangel Raphael", in which a large space of wall above the window is occupied by an intricate but rude tracery of involved quartrefoils.'

CARLO NAYA
S. Maria della Salute on the Grand Canal
Built by Baldassare Longhena, 1631-81

'*S. Maria Della Salute: one of the earliest buildings of the Grotesque Renaissance rendered impressive by its position, size, and general proportions ... An architect trained in the worst schools, and utterly devoid of all meaning and purpose in his work, may yet have such a natural gift of massing and grouping as will render all his structures effective when seen from a distance; such a gift is very general with the late Italian builders, so that many of the most contemptible edifices in the country have good stage effect so long as we do not approach them.*'

Palazzo Cavalli and Palazzo Barbaro

'These two buildings form the principal objects in the foreground of the view which almost every artist seizes on his first traverse of the Grand Canal, the Church of the Salute forming a most graceful distance. Neither is, however, of much value, except in general effect, but the Barbaro is the best.'

'The Palazzo Cavalli: An imposing pile, on the Grand Canal, of Renaissance Gothic, but of little merit in the details; and the effect of its traceries has been of late destroyed by the addition of modern external blinds. Its balconies are good, of the later Gothic type.'

CARLO NAYA

View taken from the Traghetto S. Tomà: Palazzi Rezzonico, Giustiniani & Foscari

Palazzo Rezzonico: 'Palace on the Grand Canal of the Grotesque Renaissance time, but less extravagant than usual'.

Palazzo Giustiniani: 'Next the Casa Foscari on the Grand Canal. Said to have been built by the Giustiniani family before 1428. It is one of those founded directly on the Ducal Palace, together with the Casa Foscari at its side ... This palace contains some unusually rich detached windows, full of tracery.'

Palazzo Foscari: 'The noblest example in Venice of the fifteenth century Gothic, founded on the Ducal Palace, but lately restored and spoiled, all but the stonework of the main windows.'

'For the love of Byron, I had run the risk of a fever in drawing the under-canal vaults, and the desolate and mud-buried portico of the ruined Casa Foscari.'

CARLO NAYA

Casa D'Oro

Built by Matteo Raverti and Giovanni and Bartolomeo Bon, 1424 – c.1440

'Of these roof parapets of Venice, the examples which remain [on the Ducal Palace and Casa d'Oro] differ from those of all other cities of Italy in their purely ornamental character ... merely adaptations of the light and crown-like ornaments which crest the walls of the Arabian mosque ... The decorations of the parapet were completed by attaching gilded balls of metal to the extremities of the leaves of the lilies, and of the intermediate spires, so as literally to form for the wall a diadem of silver touched upon the points with gold.'

ATTRIBUTED TO CARLO PONTI
Palazzo Dario
A late fifteenth-century building, possibly by one of the Lombardo family of architects.

'The Venetian habitually incrusted his work with nacre; he built his houses, even his meanest, as if he had been a shellfish — roughly inside, mother-of-pearl on the surface: he was content, per-force, to gather the clay of the Brenta banks, and bake it into brick for the substance of wall; but he overlaid it with the wealth of ocean, with the most precious of foreign marbles.'

CARLO PONTI

Palazzo Contarini della Scala or Dal Bovolo

Its famous spiral staircase was built by Giovanni Candi in the late fifteenth century

'In the Corte del Maltese, at S. Paternian. It has a spiral external staircase, very picturesque, but of the fifteenth century, and without merit.'

ATTRIBUTED TO CARLO NAYA

Renaissance Sculpture of the Judgment of Solomon at the north-west corner of the Ducal Palace
Possibly by Jacopo della Quercia, c.1410

Ruskin called the 'angle' sculptures of the Ducal Palace 'the very corner stones of the edifice, and in them we may expect to find the most important evidence of the feeling, as well as of the skill, of the builder ... If there was any sentiment which they themselves desired to have expressed in the principal edifice of their city, this is the place in which we may be secure of finding it legibly inscribed': At the first two angles, whose subjects are Adam and Eve and The Drunkenness of Noah, 'it is the Gothic spirit' with its 'frank confession of its own weakness that is evident'. The 'Judgment angle' reveals in its subject matter that 'the principal element in the Renaissance spirit, is the firm confidence in its own wisdom'.

CARLO NAYA

Scala dei Giganti, Palazzo Ducale

Designed by Antonio Rizzo (1484-1501). The statues of Neptune and Mars are by Sansovino.

'It was in the year 1422 that the decree passed to rebuild the palace ... and on the 27th March [1424] the first hammer was lifted up against the old palace of Ziani. That hammer stroke was the first act of the period properly called the "Renaissance". It was the knell of the architecture of Venice, — and of Venice herself.'

After the fire of 1479, reconstruction 'was entrusted to the best Renaissance architects of the close of the fifteenth and opening of the sixteenth centuries; Antonio Ricci executing the Giant's staircase, and, on his absconding with a large sum of the public money, Pietro Lombardo taking his place'.

14

CARLO NAYA
Bridge of the Rialto
Built by Antonio da Ponte, 1588

'*The best building raised in the time of the Grotesque Renaissance; very noble in its simplicity, in its proportions, and its masonry. Note especially the grand way in which the oblique archstones rest on the butments of the bridge, safe, palpably both to the sense and eye.*'

'*... the shadowy Rialto threw its colossal curve slowly forth from behind the palace of the Camerlenghi; that strange curve, so delicate, so adamantine, strong as a mountain cavern, graceful as a bow just bent; when first, before its moonlike circumference was all risen, the gondolier's cry, "Ah! Stali", struck sharp upon the ear, and the prow turned aside under the mighty cornices that half met over the narrow canal, where the splash of the water followed close and loud, ringing along the marble by the boat's side ...*'

CARLO NAYA
Ponte De' Sospiri
Built by Antonio Contino, c.1600

'The Venice of modern fiction and drama is a thing of yesterday, a mere efflorescence of decay, a
stage dream which the first ray of daylight must dissipate into dust. No prisoner, whose name is
worth remembering, or whose sorrow deserved sympathy, ever crossed that "Bridge of Sighs," which
is the centre of the Byronic ideal of Venice; no great merchant of Venice ever saw that Rialto under
which the traveller now passes with breathless interest.'

'The well-known "Bridge of Sighs", a work of no merit and of a late period, owing the interest it
possesses chiefly to its pretty name, and to the ignorant sentimentalism of Byron'.

ATTRIBUTED TO CARLO PONTI

View over rooftops along the Grand Canal looking towards the Accademia Bridge

'When first upon the traveller's sight opened the long ranges of columned palaces — each with its own boat moored at the portal — each with its image cast down, beneath its feet, upon that green pavement which every breeze broke into new fantasies of rich tessellation ... it was no marvel that the mind should be so deeply entranced by the visionary charm of a scene so beautiful and so strange, as to forget the darker truths of its history and its being. Well might it seem that such a city had owed her existence rather to the rod of the enchanter, than the fear of the fugitive; ... and that all which in nature was wild or merciless — Time and Decay, as well as the waves and the tempests — had been won to adorn her instead of to destroy, and might still spare, for ages to come, that beauty which seemed to have fixed for its throne the sands of the hour-glass as well as of the sea'.